This book
belongs to

_____

My Book About God

Bible Promises for Little Hearts

Written and Illustrated by
Kathy Arbuckle

BARBOUR
PUBLISHING, INC.
Uhrichsville, Ohio

Published by Barbour Publishing, Inc.
        P.O. Box 719
        Uhrichsville, Ohio 44683
        http://www.barbourbooks.com

ECPA Member of the
Evangelical Christian
Publishers Association

Printed in Hong Kong.

Contents

My Book About God

Beloved, let us love one another: for love is of God; and every one that loveth is born of God, and knoweth God.

1 JOHN 4:7

Where does love come from?

The Bible, God's special Book, says that God is love. He has given you so much love that you have plenty of extra love. Where can love go? Anywhere. You can share God's love with everyone around you.

My Book About God

We love Him, because He first loved us.

1 JOHN 4:19

How much does God love you?

God knew who you were before you were born. God loved you before you were born. God's love is greater than any other love. That's because no one—nothing—is greater than God.

My Book About God

The Lord preserveth all them that love Him.

PSALM 145:20

Do you love God?

Jesus told us to love God with all our heart, all our soul, and all our mind. That means you should love God with everything inside you. If you love God, God will always be with you.

My Book About God

And we know that all things work together for good to them that love God.

ROMANS 8:28

Do you love God all the time ?

Sometimes bad things happen. You may spill paint on your new dress. You may fall down outside and scrape your knees. Your friend may not want to play with you. But you should never stop loving God. Even during bad times God loves you. God will always do what is best for you.

My Book About God

For Thou, Lord, wilt bless the righteous.

PSALM 5:12

When you love God do you act differently ?

The Bible says if you love God, you do what is right. God will take care of you. God wants to be the most important part of your life.

My Book About God

And they that know Thy name will put their trust in Thee: for Thou, Lord, hast not forsaken them that seek Thee.

PSALM 9:10

What does it mean to be a best friend?

A best friend is always there when you need them. Just as the sun comes up every day, God is always there. God is stronger than anyone or anything. God is everywhere and He knows everything. God wants to be with you every day. God wants to be your best friend.

My Book About God

And ye shall eat in plenty, and be satisfied, and praise the name of the Lord your God.

JOEL 2:26

Do you thank God for your food ?

Before you eat you should close your eyes and bow your head and thank God for your food. God gives you so much to be thankful for. All of the wonderful things you have to eat come from God.

God Gives You Good Things   19

My Book About God

Behold the fowls of the air: for they sow not, neither do they reap, nor gather into barns; yet your Heavenly Father feedeth them. Are ye not much better than they?

MATTHEW 6:26

Who feeds the wild birds and animals?

You never see little sparrows going to the market to buy food. Or bears sitting in a restaurant having some breakfast. God feeds all of the wild birds and animals. But you are more important to God than all the animals. God will always take care of you.

My Book About God

And he shall be like a tree planted by the rivers of water, that bringeth forth his fruit in his season.

PSALM 1:3

Have you ever picked an apple from a tree?

God is like a gardener and you are like a tree. God makes sure you have plenty of water and sunshine to help you grow. God wants you to "bloom" and tell others about Him.

God Helps You Grow　　　23

My Book About God

The Lord is good, a strong hold in the day of trouble; and He knoweth them that trust in Him.

NAHUM 1:7

Have you ever seen a fire engine rushing to a fire?

Just like a fire engine with its sirens blaring and lights flashing, God is always ready to hurry to your side. There is no problem that is too big for Him. He is more powerful than anything or anyone in the universe. God is awesome!

My Book About God

And ye shall seek **M**e, and find **M**e, when ye shall search for **M**e with all your heart.

JEREMIAH 29:13

Do you play hide and seek ?

That's a fun game to play with your friends and family. But God does not play that game. God will never hide from you. God is always there to help you, listen to you, and most of all, to love you.

My Book About God

Blessed is that man that maketh the Lord his trust.

PSALM 40:4

Does the sun come up every morning?

That's God's way of saying, "Have a wonderful day!" You can trust God to always do what He says. You can trust God to always be there, morning, noon, and night.

My Book About God

In all thy ways acknowledge Him, and He shall direct thy paths.

PROVERBS 3:6

Have you ever tried to follow a map?

God is like a map. God will show you which way to go and what to do. Just ask Him to help you. Let God be your map.

God Is Like a Map

My Book About God

Thy Word is a lamp unto my feet, and a light unto my path.

PSALM 119:105

Have you ever tried to find your way in the dark?

You probably bumped into furniture. Maybe you even fell down! When you don't know where you're going, or what to do, you can read God's special Book, the Bible. God will speak to you through His Words. God will keep you from falling down.

My Book About God

All scripture is given by inspiration of God, and is profitable for doctrine, for reproof, for correction, for instruction in righteousness: That the man of God may be perfect. 2 TIMOTHY 3:16,17

Why is it important to follow directions?

If you don't, you won't be able to finish a project. The Bible is a big book of important directions. If you follow God's directions, you will be happy your whole life.

My Book About God

Thou shalt make thy prayer unto Him, and He shall hear thee.

JOB 22:27

Do you ever need to talk to God?

When you talk to God, you are praying to Him. God loves to hear your prayers! He is always there to listen to you. No matter where you are, God can hear you. You can ask God for help for yourself or someone else. You can thank God for His goodness and tell Him how much you love Him.

My Book About God

Wait on the Lord: be of good courage, and He shall strengthen thine heart: wait, I say, on the Lord.

PSALM 27:14

Will God answer your prayers right away?

Not always. Sometimes God has a special reason to wait. He knows what will happen in the future. God knows the best time to answer your prayers. Wait for God to do things His way, the best way.

My Book About God

For Thou art my hope, O Lord God: Thou art my trust from my youth.

PSALM 71:5

Have you ever been so sad you just can't get happy again?

Sometimes everything around you seems bad. When that happens you can tell God everything that is bothering you. You can pray. God will always hear you. God will always love you.

My Book About God

And she shall bring forth a son, and thou shalt call His name Jesus: for He shall save His people from their sins.

MATTHEW 1:21

Whose birthday do you celebrate at Christmas?

Jesus' birthday, the birthday of God's only Son! Long ago God's Son Jesus lived on the earth. He was put to death on a cross and was buried. Three days later Jesus came alive again! Jesus died and came alive again because He loves you. Jesus "paid the price" for everything bad you think or do. Because of Jesus, after you die you will live forever in heaven. Heaven is God's home.

44   *My Book About God*

And this is the record, that God hath given to us eternal life, and this life is in His Son.

I JOHN 5:11

What is eternal life ?

When you have eternal life you are able to live forever. If you believe that Jesus is God's Son, one day you will go to heaven. You will live in heaven eternally, forever. Even though no one knows exactly what heaven is like, we do know God's home is the most beautiful place you could imagine.

My Book About God

Therefore if any man be in Christ, he is a new creature.

2 CORINTHIANS 5:17

Have you ever seen a butterfly come out of its coccoon?

Did you know that you are like a butterfly? When you say you believe in Jesus, you have become a new person. Now you will live your life to please God. Someday your earthly body will die. But, just like a butterfly, you will fly up to heaven. There you will live with God and all your family and friends who love God. Remember, God loves you forever!

And He took them up in His arms, put His hands upon them, and blessed them.

MARK 10:16